Merge
A Guidebook for Youth Service Trips
By Krista Dutt

Merge: A Guidebook for Youth Service Trips
By Krista Dutt

The publisher expresses deep appreciation for the time, expertise, and support the
DOOR Network gave to this project. Discovering Opportunities for Outreach and
Reflection (DOOR) is a faith based network of urban service-learning programs that
expose, educate, challenge, and motivate participants to respond to the issues and
concerns of an urban context. Program offerings range from a weekend to a year and
include opportunities for individuals and groups. www.doornetwork.org

International Standard Book Number: 978-0-8361-9488-3

Design by Reuben Graham

Printed in USA

Orders and information:
USA: 800-245-7894
Canada: 800-631-6535
www.mpn.net

CONTENTS

INTRODUCTION

You have decided to lead a service learning trip. Good for you! Your trip may have come into being as a result of an invitation from a sister church in another state or province (or even country), or from some intentional planning and option-checking on your part. In any case, you're looking for ways to get the most meaning out of the experience. I trust that this guide, with its Bible helps, group-building suggestions, and practical advice will be help you and your group have a satisfying experience.

This guide uses the story of Moses and his family as the biblical foundation for topics you will cover in this journey: 1) team building; 2) spiritual growth; 3) diversity; 4) joining in God's work; 5) service; 6) reflection; and 7) action. I suggest that you, the leader, read the entire book of Exodus in order to have a constant reminder of the larger story. All the while, think of the parallels between your group's service experience and the experience of Israel.

Merge may sound like a strange title for this book. But it was intentionally chosen, and not just because of all the "merge" signs you will see on the highways you travel. For Christian believers, a life of service is all about joining God's work in history. God is active in the world, healing, restoring, and bringing in God's *shalom* through Christ. God has brought light into our own lives. In response, we merge our wills and our energies with God's, allowing ourselves to be instruments of God's peace.

The guide is organized into seven parts, each with reproducible handouts. The first four are sessions of preparation—before you go on your trip. They will help build your service group into a team and become spiritually prepared. The fifth "session" is one that may take different forms, depending on the circumstances of your trip. It offers opportunities to consult and reflect while you are in the thick of your service assignment. The sixth and seventh sessions come after the trip is over. They will help your team reflect on the trip and begin integrating what they learned into their daily lives.

As a part of your participants' faith development, each session uses various spiritual disciplines to help your group be aware of God's work in them—and in the world they are serving. Times of silence, prayer, music, service, and celebration will help participants be mindful of God's call. (For more information about spiritual disciplines, missional theology, and other topics, see the list of resources on page 65.)

An important part of your group's experience will be the practice of journaling. At the back of this book are journal pages with reflection questions. Copy and assemble these pages into booklets that your group can use on their own and, on the trip itself, during your group reflection times. The journal will not only provide a record of the experience, but also help your participants interact with the Bible and their experiences before, during, and after the trip.

This guide is meant to make the preparation and follow-up easier for you. However, you the leader will still need to invest quality time in the experience. Be sure to read this introduction well in advance of your planning, and leave enough time to work through the session planning that you're not caught in a mad scramble.

OVERVIEW OF THE SESSIONS

Here, in more detail, is a session-by-session preview of the guide, with a few practical things to keep in mind from the outset. These summaries are followed by a planning timetable and a list of practical tips.

To give the sessions the time they need, plan at least an hour per session—two if possible. Suggested times for a one-hour setting are included for each activity within the session. Be prepared to adapt them to the time you have. There are also suggestions for optional or additional activities that require more time and sometimes, different settings.

BEFORE SESSION 1

Meet with your fellow leaders to establish your goals for the trip. Some groups focus on the team-building aspects of service-learning experiences; others emphasize the service or the cross cultural learning. You need to figure out what your group needs and wants. Team building and bonding is the focus of Session 1 and it will happen no matter what, but if this is your main goal you should plan for even more team building activities than what are offered in the curriculum.

SESSION 1—TRUST: BUILDING A TEAM

Whether your group has known each other for awhile or just met, it is important to develop a team identity for the approaching trip. If your group is just getting acquainted, you may want to use more icebreakers. A quick Google search for "icebreakers" will turn up more ideas than you can count. The team of Moses, Aaron, Zipporah, and Miriam will be highlighted in this session as models for your own team. You will also invite a congregational "Jethro" to participate, representing your home support base.

A team covenant will be written in this session. In the Bible text, the people of God are invited to live out their covenant relationships with God, others, and the world. Your covenant will have a similar function; it is a shared agreement, an active tool to keep a team focused on common goals and accountable to them.

The session also includes choosing a theme song. If you are not a singing group, a recording could work.

SESSION 2—INNER LIFE: PREPARING TO MEET GOD

There are so many practical sides to serving-learning trips that it's easy to forget the importance of building one's faith before departure. Moses' experience with the burning bush, the focus for this session, highlights the centrality of God's call and involvement in our lives.

As leader, remember that you are not only guiding others during this trip; you also may be in for some transformative spiritual change as well. Noting your dual role of leader and participant is important. Consider meeting separately with sponsors and other leaders after each session and during the trip to work through your own change and growth.

Since this session is based on the story of the burning bush, I suggest a creative visual of a "burning bush" for your worship center. Consider asking someone in your congregation, or in the team itself, to create this display.

Session 3—Awareness: Understanding culture

Whether your trip takes you across town or across the country, your team will likely cross cultural boundaries. The biblical focus, therefore, is Moses' bi-cultural identity. Your group is encouraged to do a study of your home area and of the community where you will be serving. For this, be in contact *as soon as possible* with local leaders and/ or hosts for information about the area that you will soon visit.

Cross cultural experiences can be difficult to navigate and even harder to discuss. It is especially important for you as leader to work through the cultural awareness exercises well ahead of time. And in the session itself, don't give up too soon if conversation lags. Encourage participants to identify their understandings of different cultures and then ask why? Note also that the activities suggest that you invite visitors, probably from the congregation, to speak about working cross-culturally and/ or to help lead the singing. The session also offers an extender activity that explores racism and white privilege.

Session 4—God's Activity: Joining God's mission

The sessions till now have been about team-building, faith, and cultural awareness. This session moves toward action. While Session 5 will occur during the actual trip, this session hopes to get participants asking themselves, "How am I joining God's work in the world?"

As leader, you may find it hard in your busy life to model the practice of listening to God. Each day that you are with the group (especially on the trip) take time to think through the ways you have joined God's work and ask participants to do the same. Help model respect and excitement for the work that God is doing in the destination as well as at home.

Especially in the "Responding" section, time restraints may force you to choose between the two activities offered, so plan well ahead. The first, an interview with a congregation member who approaches his or her work with a missional mindset, should be used if your group hasn't been exposed to many models of service and mission. If you use this option, invite the visitor well in advance.

The second activity should be given priority if the youth are inclined to see God's work as only "out there"—for example, at your trip destination—and not right at home where they are. It involves moving your meeting venue.

Session 5—Faith in action (the actual service trip)

This "session" is actually six gatherings during your trip; if your trip is a different length, modify as you see fit. The materials include guidelines for group journaling and reflective activities. Using the activities may not be necessary if you are serving with an organization that provides such input as part of their hosting, but you can still adapt them. You should especially consider arranging time for the action plans on Day 6.

Whether or not you have time for all the activities, the journaling will be important components of your team's experience. Each day's page includes the Bible text to read, a short paragraph referring to the text, and questions for the youth to consider. If possible, work through these pages together; read the text, take a few moments of quiet individual reflection, and talk and pray together.

The reflective activities give further opportunities for group reflection and bonding. Be sure to look over the plan for these activities well ahead of time. The following items need some advance thought and preparation:

- Review the team covenant (Day 3). This is a time to address any conflict within the group. The faster conflicts are dealt with in an open manner, the sooner participants can get back to serving and learning.

- Write postcards to the congregation (Day 4). This not only provides opportunities for reflection, but also offers connection to the home congregation, especially your "Jethros."

- Serve the "Bread of Life" (Day 5). For the ritual, use bread that represents the host community (e.g. pita bread, if you are in the Middle East).

- Take good notes. Jot down your thoughts and decisions. Especially on Day 6, your decisions on action goals will become part of your team work following the trip.

SESSION 6—REFLECTION: WHAT DID WE JUST DO?

For a service trip to be meaningful, participants need to take time to think about what they experienced. This session highlights the Israelites' entry into the Promised Land, their new home. In crossing the Jordan River, they remind themselves of God's dramatic journey with them across the Red Sea and through the wilderness The participants, too, will cross over a symbolic Jordan River, so start thinking early about how that might work in your space.

As leader, take time to do your own reflection on the trip. Share the experience with your team of leaders, your friends, and your family. Make sure you also work through the one-word exercise and the action steps mentioned in Session 5 before this session. Be open with participants, but be careful of taking over the time reflecting about your own experience.

In the group reflection activities (through the scrapbook and the review of action steps from Session 5), your team will keep up the momentum of your trip and lay the groundwork for new directions. The activities require some careful forethought and planning, especially for the options that require other venues.

SESSION 7—INTEGRATION: WHAT TO DO WITH WHAT WE LEARNED

Trips can be mountaintop experiences, but often we tumble down to the valley soon after we arrive home. The song of Miriam will help your group further process what they learned on the trip and then to move into the future. This session gives you opportunity to work further with your action goals, and to make plans for further follow up.

The closing activity encourages the group to revisit their trip experience on a regular basis. I recommend this be done for a year, on the month-anniversaries of the trip. Check the ideas listed in the session and think ahead to how you see this happening.

A BLESSING

My hope for you is that by walking with your service group in trust, faith, awareness, action, reflection, and integration you find yourself spiritually energized and merging with God's work. Blessings on the journey!

Krista Dutt

A PLANNING TIMETABLE FOR YOUR TRIP

The following timeline assumes you will be planning a summer trip, but it can be adapted for a trip at other times (such as spring break). The important thing is that you keep in mind the long work of preparation that goes in to planning an effective service and learning experience.

September and October: Research locations and programs that are available to you. (See pages 67-68 for some starters.) If you go with a pre-packaged program, contact and ask the organizers about their views on important elements of the trip. If you wish to worship at a local church, for example, make sure the program has that available.

October and November: Sign up for an arranged program or make arrangements for trip. Start to get the word out in your congregation. Set deadlines for deposits and payments with youth and parents.

January: Determine the leadership for the trip. Make sure adult leaders have vacation available for this time, and if they have children, they can arrange childcare. Invite them to all pre-trip meetings.

February: Start thinking about transportation. Are you flying? Driving? Borrowing or renting a van? Also, work through advance planning for the sessions you will conduct before your trip.
- Read through this guide and note the arrangements that need more than a couple of weeks of planning:
- Determine if you need to have extra sessions following Sessions 3 and 7.
- Decide who your congregation's "Jethro" supporters (Session 1) will be.
- Research the culture of your destination (Session 3).
- Invite your special guests (Sessions 1, 3, 4, 6, and 7).

Six weeks before departure: Begin your sessions with the group. You'll do Sessions 1 through 4 before departure and 5 during the trip.

March-June: Finalize plans with the on-site leaders at your service location. Be in communication with the other trip leaders from your congregation.

One week before trip: Distribute packing lists and weather information. Make sure the youth understand what to bring and not to bring, based on what you've heard from your hosts.

After the trip: Keep up the momentum by celebrating what you learned and following up on action goals. In Sessions 6 and 7, you are encouraged to invite parents, congregational leaders, and others who were part of your support group, to join you as you remember the trip and integrate what you learned.

Three months after trip: Evaluate progress in your action goals.

Six months after trip: Mark the completion of action goals, and evaluate ones that are still being implemented.

One year after trip: Host a reunion for the team. Review action steps and start planning another trip.

PRACTICAL IDEAS FOR LEADING THE TRIP

- **Be aware of your goals for the trip.** Pray that your intentions merge with God's purposes rather than serve your own agenda.

- **Be in contact with local leaders before you arrive.** Find out what you are in charge of and what they will do. (For example, DOOR provides service projects, speakers, meals and reflection resources.) Be sure to state your requests. If you want to spend time together in your group, and I hope you do, ask when there is time to do this. If you want to see a baseball game, ask if there is free time; don't assume that you can just skip programming.

- When you sign up, **ask the local leaders or program director how they would like to receive money.** If you are sending checks, use the memo line for the date you are arriving.

- **The local leaders may send a packing list or give other instructions about your arrival and stay.** Please respect these instructions. If the packing list says to bring long pants, please have your participants bring long pants, even if the forecast calls for warm weather.

- **Read everything that the local leaders ask you to.** If you have questions, please ask.

- **Take time before you arrive to study a map of the area, along with the specific directions from the local leaders.** Being confident will put you and the local leader at ease.

- **Check the weather report.** Pack for the weather. Participants can find it hard to participate in activities if they are too cold or too hot.

- **Be flexible!** As much as local leaders may have planned, circumstances may change. Service sites have changing needs almost every day; and local leaders will know how to deal with them. If things seem unorganized, take a breath and be glad someone else is worrying about the details.

- **Be ready for conflict within your group**. Set aside time (as mentioned in Day 3, Session 5) to air concerns. The more open people are the less the conflict will color the experience.

- **As leaders, come with a teachable spirit.** Even while leading, you can model learning for the group.

- **Be prepared to have fun.**

SESSION 1
TRUST
BUILDING A TEAM

GOAL

Build a solid team identity for the upcoming trip.

OBJECTIVES

- Lead several team-building exercises
- Answer the question of why teams are important.
- Provide a solid biblical basis for your team to function well on the trip.

SCRIPTURE TEXT

Exodus 4:18-31

PREPARATION

SUPPLIES ✓
- ☐ A bag of candy (Opening option 1)
- ☐ Flip chart or white board with markers
- ☐ Large sheet of chart or poster paper
- ☐ Journals copied for each participant
- ☐ A pencil or pen for each participant
- ☐ Copy of the Jethro monologue (page 15)
- ☐ A collection of lyrics and music from which to choose a group song.
  Some suggestions: Chris Rice's "Face of Christ"; Casey Corum's "Dwell"; Anointed's "The Call"; Miami Music Ministry's "Love Found You"; or songs found in *Hymnal: A Worship Book* such as 546, "Guide My Feet"; 6, "Gather Us In"; or 439, "I want Jesus to Walk With Me."
- ☐ CD and player

Tasks ✓

- ❑ If you haven't done so already, read the Introduction (page 4) to get a solid sense of where this curriculum is taking you.
- ❑ Copy the journal pages (page 54) and staple them into booklets, one per youth.
- ❑ Copy the Jethro monologue (page 15).
- ❑ Get the flip chart or white board ready.
- ❑ Write these words on the chart paper: *Vision, Goals, Relationships, Attitudes.*
- ❑ Prepare materials for the icebreakers that you have picked.
- ❑ Ask a lay leader in your congregation to visit your group and perform the Scripture reading and "Jethro monologue." This person should have a grasp of the whole story of Moses. He or she should be someone the class would consider a "Jethro" who, while not traveling with the group, will encourage the group on this path of service.
- ❑ Review several options for the team song and be ready to present them.

Session

Opening (10 minutes)
Choose one of the following two icebreakers.

Option 1: The candy game
1. Pass around the bag of candy with this warning: *You can take as many as you like as long as they fit in one hand. And do not eat them yet.*
2. Once all have candy, say: *For each piece of candy you have, tell us one sentence about yourself.* [If you are a large group, you may need to limit the number people sharing.]

Option 2: Stories from childhood
Ask everyone to partner with someone they don't know very well. Then, in pairs, take turns telling a story from their kindergarten year.

After the exercise, open the session with a prayer in a style that is familiar to the group. The following model covers many of the themes of the upcoming course.

> *God, we're at the beginning of an amazing adventure. Over the next weeks, we'll be forming ourselves into a team, learning about your ways, growing in our personal relationship with you, and getting involved in service in a different place. Walk with us on this journey. Open our eyes to see, strengthen our hands and feet to do your work, and send us the joy of your Spirit. Amen.*

FOCUSING (10 MINUTES)
How do you make a peanut butter and jelly sandwich?

The following exercise helps to show that people process and create things differently. In pairs, have the youth describe in detail the way they make a peanut butter and jelly sandwich. They should include how much of each they use, whether they use butter as well, whether they mix the jam with the peanut butter, how they cut the sandwich, etc.

Then, in the large group, ask:
- Did you assume that your partner would make it just like you did?
- Did you think your partner made the sandwich in the wrong way?
- Is there something that you liked about your partner's description that you would like to adopt in the way you make a sandwich?
- What does this exercise tell us about how teams work together?

Indicate that you will come back to similar questions later in the session, when you talk about covenant.

TELLING THE BIBLICAL STORY (5-7 MINUTES)
Say something like: *On this service and learning experience, we will form a team. That means we will try to exercise good communication skills and open ourselves to learning, and to growth as we travel and work together. In the Bible, Moses and some of his family members formed a team with a special mission: to lead the people of Israel out of Egypt to the Promised Land. We are going to use their journey as a model for our own. Let's listen to Moses' story to hear about the formation of his team.*

Your "Jethro" now reads Exodus 4:18-31, followed by the dramatic monologue (page 15).

EXPLORING THE STORY (10 MINUTES)
Discuss:
- What sticks out to you in this text? Why?
- How important is Jethro in the story? What's his role?
- Where does Aaron fit into this story?
- From what you know of the larger Moses story, how does this story fit in the larger story of the people of Israel? How well did Moses' agenda merge with God's purposes?

Give a short talk based on the following:
Moses gets all the attention in the stories of the Exodus. Moses is the star on the team. When I read Exodus, I can almost hear people shouting, "Moses! Moses! He's our man! If he can't do it no one can!"

And yet, if we read the story carefully, we can see that he has supporters, teammates, and people who care for him along the way. Moses isn't alone. When he is a baby, Moses' mother protects him from Pharaoh's massacre of Hebrew babies by floating him down the river in a basket, to be found by Egyptian women. Miriam, his sister, cares for Moses by helping Pharaoh's daughter find a proper nurse for Moses. When Moses leaves Egypt, he finds hospitality with Jethro, the priest of Midian, whose daughter Zipporah later becomes his wife. Aaron, Moses' brother, is also called to speak on behalf of Moses.

Moses receives Jethro's blessing for this journey in God's service. He travels with Zipporah, Aaron, and probably Miriam, to start a new journey in God's service. While the story tells us that Moses accepts this call from God, the people around him also must feel a similar call. Each person's sense of purpose is equally important and helps the team to function.

Each person has a role to play. Even though Jethro doesn't actually travel with Moses, he does bless Moses to live into God's call for his life. He likely gives Moses food and travel provisions for the way. In other words, Jethro gives practical as well as emotional support for the journey.

Zipporah, Moses' wife, doesn't come along just for the ride. When Moses is threatened, she saves not only him but the family. Zipporah watches out for the whole group. It seems she has a gift of quick thinking and remembers the practical things. Zipporah might have been the one to say to the rest of the team, "Hey, we have been walking for five hours, and I know we are all excited to get to Pharaoh's house, but maybe we should stop for stretch break so we don't get a cramp."

Aaron is brought into the team for a specific skill. It is clear from Exodus 3 that Moses has little confidence in public speaking; Aaron becomes the go-to guy for speech-making. Leaning on Aaron for this skill set allows Moses to use his skills in other ways.

Miriam is not mentioned in today's story as a key member of this team, but some Bible scholars think she was likely a part of the group. From the later story of Miriam's leadership of the Israelites' victory song (Exodus 15), she keeps everyone focused. She is willing to do all sorts of tasks, from watching over her brother when he is a baby, to celebrating God's work with a song. Now, as she joins the team, we can imagine her becoming the multi-tasker for the team, the versatile one.

As we learn later in the story, Moses' team is far from perfect, but it is a team. Just as experience draws the Exodus team together, our team will be drawn together through our experience together. This is the group that you will start this journey with. This will be the group of people that will understand the joke that you make up at the service site. This will be the group that you serve and serve with. This will be the group that will understand why you come home with different attitudes.

RESPONDING TO THE STORY (20-25 MINUTES)
1. Team covenant
Brainstorm answers to the following questions, writing the group's answers on the large poster paper, under the headings: VISION, GOALS, RELATIONSHIPS, ATTITUDES:
- What is our vision for this trip?
- What are specific goals we should have?
- What are some God-honoring ways we can to treat one another while we are traveling and serving?
- What kinds of attitudes do we need to have toward one another?

Once you have 15 to 20 statements posted, go through them again and ask the participants which ones may not reflect the feelings of the entire group. Remove, combine, alter, and add to the list. Make sure words such as *accountability* and *evaluation* are included.

When you've agreed upon a list of ten to twelve statements, these will become the covenant that will guide your trip. Write them on the poster board and have all participants sign it.

Note that in each session you will review this covenant to make sure it reflects your goals for the trip. As you learn new things, you may need to tweak it. By the time you depart for your trip, this covenant should be a solid guiding document while you are doing your service.

2. Journals

Conduct a conversation with the group about journaling and blogging.

- How many of you journal? Why?
- How many of you blog? Why?

Distribute journals. Explain that a key part of this learning/serving experience will be the personal journals that each youth will keep. The journal will help them sort out what they are experiencing before, during, and after the trip. It will also be a souvenir that they can keep for reference.

Stress that the youth should bring their journals to each session (especially Sessions 3 and 6) and that they will also be a key part of the trip itself. Encourage the youth to do their journaling on the same day of the session, while group discussions are fresh in their minds.

Journals should be written on their own time, but occasionally the youth will have time to work on them during the session. If you have time, take a few moments for everyone to answer the first question for this session.

3. Theme song

Suggest to the group that you would like to decide on a theme song for this trip. Suggest the titles of several songs, and either play recordings of them or sing them. Come to a consensus on which will be your song.

CLOSING (5 MINUTES)
Prayer

Ask five people from the group to pray for the study and trip experience, each focusing on the different roles that will be played:

- Jethro, the one who stays at home and blesses the group
- Moses, the leader
- Zipporah the practical person
- Aaron the speaker
- Miriam, the multi-tasker and celebration person.

If your group is uncomfortable with spontaneous prayers, lead this time yourself.

PREPARATION FOR NEXT TIME

Ask each person to bring an object that represents a time when God was present to them.

THE JETHRO MONOLOGUE

Based on Exodus 4:18-23, 27-31

After being my son-in-law for a few years, Moses came to me and said, "Please let me go back to my kindred in Egypt and see whether they are still living."

I told him, "Go in peace."

I know that God and Moses were in direct contact. According to Moses, he had received instructions from God directly. So what choice did I have? Moses, my son-in-law, was to go back to Egypt to challenge Pharaoh. I watched as Moses, my daughter, Zipporah, and my grandkids packed up and left to go to Egypt.

Again, the Lord spoke to Moses and said, "When you go back to Egypt, see that you perform before Pharaoh all the wonders that I have put in your power; but I will harden his heart, so that he will not let the people go."

Then Moses was to tell Pharaoh, 'Thus says the Lord: Israel is my firstborn son. I said to you, "Let my son go that he may worship me." But you refused to let him go; now I will kill your firstborn son.'"

What a call my son-in-law had!

I found out, around the same time, that the Lord said to Aaron, Moses' brother, "Go into the wilderness to meet Moses."

So Aaron went; and he met Moses and the rest of the family at the mountain of God. Moses told Aaron about all the words he had received from the Lord, and all the signs God had showed him.

Then Moses and Aaron assembled all the elders of the Israelites. Aaron spoke the words that the Lord had spoken to Moses, and performed the signs in the sight of the people.

The people believed; and when they heard that the Lord had given heed to the Israelites and that he had seen their misery, they bowed down and worshipped.

What a call Moses' family has!

SESSION 2
INNER LIFE
PREPARING TO MEET GOD

GOAL

Encourage the team of the need to be spiritually prepared for the trip.

OBJECTIVES

- Offer team members the opportunity to share experiences where God has met them.
- Provide a biblical foundation for recognizing the way God prepares them for service.
- Help the group understand their expectations for the trip.

SCRIPTURE TEXT

Exodus 3:1-12

PREPARATION

SUPPLIES ✓

- ❏ Flip chart or white board with markers
- ❏ Copies of "Facing the I AM God" reader's theatre (page 21)
- ❏ Materials to create a "burning bush," such as a large pillar light, several tea light candles, fire-colored fabric or paper, sticks, and matches or lighter.
- ❏ Worship display area with space to add the "burning bush"
- ❏ A smaller candle for each person
- ❏ The objects that the youth will have brought, as requested in Session 1
- ❏ A group of objects (one per person) that are incomplete: a pizza with everything but cheese, Oreos™ with the cream scraped out, pitcher of water without a glass, a portable game player without batteries. Each item should be in individual bags or containers to conceal that they are missing something (Responding).
- ❏ A computer with access to the Internet, to show a Facebook page (if possible, with an LCD projector to show it larger). If this is not possible, bring a paper copy of a blank Facebook® profile page.
- ❏ Sheets of paper (11x14 inches), one per person
- ❏ Colored markers
- ❏ A copy of Nichole Nordeman's "Small Enough" CD, along with a CD player; or have copies of the lyrics (available at http://www.christianlyricsonline.com/artists/nichole-nordeman/small-enough.html).

TASKS ✓

- ☐ Ask four group members to perform the reader's theatre, and arrange a time to practice it.
- ☐ Prepare the objects for use in Responding option 1.
- ☐ Set up the flip chart and markers. If you plan to do the Facebook® activity (Responding 2), post the questions found in that section on the chart paper.
- ☐ Create a worship display area that includes a "burning bush." Suggestion: scrunch up orange, red, and yellow fabric or paper under some sticks, and place small tea lights in glass containers around the fire. Use the pillar candle to represent the Christ light.
- ☐ Set up the computer and, if possible, an LCD projector.
- ☐ Look up lyrics for "Small Enough" or cue your CD player to play the recording.

SESSION

OPENING (5 MINUTES)

Welcome the group.

Ask participants to have ready the object you asked them to bring at the end of Session 1. Explain that during the opening prayer exercise, each will have an opportunity to prayerfully remember an experience when they felt close to God. They will say in a sentence or two what the moment was and how the object represents that moment.

If some youth have left their object at home, they may share without their object. Others may not feel they have felt close to God, or would rather not share; if so, don't force the sharing.

FOCUSING (10 MINUTES)

Start with a prayer something like this:

God of the burning bush, sometimes you get our attention with fire, sometimes with grains of sand. We thank you for knowing what we need and when we need it. We remember those times that you have become near to us in the past. Amen.

Invite youth to share. After each person shares, say, "*We thank you, God, for coming near to _____ (name of participant)'s life.*" If the person has not felt close to God, say: "*God, we thank you for _____ 's journey with you.*"

When all have finished sharing, close with prayer: *God, keep us attentive to the many ways that you come into our lives each day. Amen.*

TELLING THE BIBLICAL STORY (5 MINUTES)

Say: *Encountering God can be a wonderful spiritual experience. It can also be jarring, and spiritual growth isn't always what we think it might be. Listen for Moses' thoughts in the passage today.*

Have the four readers present the Scripture text using the readers theatre, "Facing the I AM God," based on Exodus 3.

EXPLORING THE STORY (10 MINUTES)

Discuss the following:

- What role does the burning bush have in the story?
- What is the significance of "I am who I am" as the name of God?
- How is Moses' role defined in this passage?
- What choice does Moses have in accepting God's call?

Adapt the following thoughts on the text. Try to make it more of a conversation than a lecture.

Have you ever walked into a book discussion ready to have a moving discussion, but you didn't bother to read the book? Have you ever sat down to write a paper that is due the next day but requires footnotes and at least ten resources, only to realize that you haven't done any research? Have you or your family traveled to a holiday destination only to find that all the hotels were booked?

Often people come to a service learning trip thinking, "I will just show up and be changed." While God's spirit can change us, we can easily miss that opportunity if we aren't prepared. Moses doesn't just show up in front of Pharaoh one day, hoping for the best. Rather, he builds on past experiences with God in order to be ready for what he knows is coming.

In the story we heard, Moses sees the burning bush and hears the voice of God calling him back to Egypt to help liberate the people from slavery. Moses then takes time to process God's words and gather a team who will be there in the next steps. With them, Moses will make this trip to Egypt, bring the Hebrew people out of slavery, and journey through the wilderness with them. Through it all, he regularly speaks to God—sometimes struggling, and sometimes just plain angry, but always responding out of his close relationship with God.

Taking the time to prepare for our service for God and to nurture our relationship with God is important for any mission venture. One youth group learned the importance of preparation while on a serving and learning trip to Chicago. Their preparation ahead of time had trained them to look for God in unlikely places. One participant told the leader that she was reminded of God in the grass growing in the cracks of the sidewalks. When the leader asked her to explain, she said, "God places us and allows us to grow in places that no one would say was even possible." While we might not all come to that conclusion, looking for God is never a dull or obsolete habit.

Being in relationship with God also means that we aren't necessarily searching for mountaintop experiences. Rather, we want to follow and be with God every day. In our story, Moses and his team are in this for the long haul. Their mission isn't just about showing up in an exotic place (Egypt); it's also about what happens when the Hebrew people are released from slavery. Preparing for both parts of the journey beforehand allows Moses' team to stay grounded in God's faithfulness.

In the same way, the service experience that we are preparing for is one stop on a longer journey of faith, both before and after the service experience. The experience of Moses tells us that God will see us through the whole journey.

RESPONDING TO THE STORY (35 MINUTES)

If possible, do both activities. If time is an issue, choose the activity that best fits your needs as you prepare for the service experience.

1. Naming our expectations

This activity helps participants understand their assumptions and expectations about the trip. To begin this reflection, the group will name the "incomplete" parts of the items that you hand out.

> Say: *I have something for each person. I have pizza, Oreos™, water, and even a Gameboy®. Who would like what?* Hand out each object. For the water object, spill it in the person's hands (the cup is the missing element).

Once the objects are distributed, the youth should be making comments like "It's not an Oreo™ unless it has cream" or "This doesn't have batteries; what good is a Gameboy® without batteries?" In response, ask these questions of purpose:

* Why does pizza have to have cheese?
* I asked if you wanted water, and I gave it to you—why did you assume that I would give you a cup?
* Is a Gameboy® a Gameboy® if it doesn't have batteries?

Then ask the following connecting questions:

* Did I lie to any of you?
* Then why would you become upset?

> Say something like: *Assumptions and expectations are real. You assumed that pizza would have cheese; you assumed that Oreos™ would have cream; and you expected that the Gameboy® would have batteries. We also have ideas of what we think might happen on a trip like the one we are planning.*

Have youth share what they assume or expect will happen on their upcoming trip, writing their thoughts on the flip chart or white board. After a few suggestions, ask them to categorize the expectations under headings such as *fun*, *spiritual growth*, *learning*, etc.

Discuss:

* Are these reasonable expectations?
* If so, what can we do to make sure these expectations are fulfilled?
* If not, how can we adjust our expectations?
* What will happen if these expectations aren't met?

2. If God had a Facebook® account . . .

This activity is meant to help participants think about their understandings of God.

> Ask: *Who has a Facebook® account? Does your profile describe who you are? What is important for people to note on your profile? In the next few moments you are going to create a Facebook® page for God.*

Distribute the paper and markers. Ask youth to think about what would be in God's photo album, what God's update would be in the last ten days, etc. When everyone has completed the profile, have the youth form into pairs to discuss the following questions (posted on chart paper):

- Why did you choose the features you did?
- Who are God's Facebook® friends?
- What extra features of Facebook® does God use? Why?

Option

If your group isn't well versed in Facebook®, have each youth describe or draw a picture that they might find on God's living room wall. They should feel free to use words and pictures. Then, in pairs, they will each ask their partner:

- How do you envision this fitting into God's living room?
- What are the most significant pieces of the picture?
- What do you learn about God from this?

Closing (10 minutes)

Refer to the group covenant. Identify goals and visions that have been answered during this session. Then repeat your covenant together and play or sing your group song.

Then gather around your "burning bush" worship area. Give each person a small candle, and light the candles that make up your burning bush, including the Christ candle. Announce that you will pray using music, silent time, and candles, and that you will cue them when to share their thoughts out loud, if they are willing. There will be times of silence when no one is sharing Tell them that you will alert them when to add their candles to the worship area.

Pray, *God of large ideas and small details, we come to you.* [Play "Small Enough" or read the lyrics, followed by a few moments of silence. If you do not use the song, just enjoy the silence.]

Creating God, you provided a burning bush for Moses. You provided an angel for those in the fiery furnace. You provided a limp for Jacob as a reminder of his wrestle with you. In surprising and big ways, you have marked your desires for your people. We think out loud or in silence of the big ways that you have found us, marked us. [Allow time for spontaneous sharing and silence.]

Creating God, you have also provided the small details of life. A tree limb so Zaccheus could see Jesus, wine for a wedding celebration, and friends to carry an ill man to Jesus. We think out loud or in silence of the ways we find you in the details of everyday life. [Allow spontaneous sharing and silence.]

Creating God, you are in the large and the small of life. As we think about where you are sending us and what you are calling us to do, we bring the light you have given each of us to your all consuming bright fire. [Leave some silence, and then invite participants to come and light their candles and set them around the burning bush.] *Amen.*

Preparation for next time:

Remind the group of the journal pages, and encourage them to take time to write their thoughts. Ask them to bring their journals to the next session.

FACING THE I AM GOD

Based on Exodus 3

1: Moses was tending the flock of his father-in-law Jethro, the priest of Midian. He came to Horeb, the mountain of God. There the angel of the Lord appeared to him in a flame of fire out of a bush. He looked, and the bush was blazing, yet it was not consumed.

2: Then Moses said,

3: Hey! There is a fire! Why isn't it spreading?

1: When Moses had turned aside to see, the Lord called to him out of the bush,

4: Moses, Moses!

2: And Moses said,

3: What?! Who's that? Who is talking to me?

2: Then God said,

4: Come no closer! Remove the sandals from your feet, for the place on which you are standing is holy ground. I am the God of your parents. I am the God of Abraham and Sarah, Isaac and Rebekah, and Jacob and Rachel.

1: And Moses hid his face, for he was afraid to look at God.

2: Then the Lord said,

4: I have observed the misery of my people in Egypt; I have heard their cry on account of their taskmasters. I know their sufferings, and I have come down to deliver them from the Egyptians. I will bring them up out of that land to a good and broad land, a land flowing with milk and honey, to the country of the Canaanites and the Hittites, and other tribes. The cry of the Israelites has now come to me; I have also seen how the Egyptians oppress them. So come, I will send you to Pharaoh to bring my people, the Israelites, out of Egypt.

2: But Moses said to God,

3: And I am supposed to be the one who does that? Right! I was raised in Pharaoh's house—remember? Now, I'm supposed to challenge him?

2: And God said,

4: I will be with you; and this shall be the sign that it is I who sent you: when you have brought the people out of Egypt, you shall worship God on this mountain.

2: But Moses said to God,

3: Okay, if I choose to accept this mission, and I say, "The God of my ancestors sent me," they are going to ask for more details. Can you at least give me your actual name?

2: God said to Moses,

4: I AM WHO I AM. Thus you shall say to the Israelites, "I AM has sent me to you. The God of your ancestors, Abraham and Sarah, Isaac and Rebekah, and Jacob and Rachel, has sent me to you. This is my name for all generations."

3: So, not only do you want me to convince Pharaoh—you also aren't going to have a burning bush for the Israelites? Really, God? What if they don't accept me?

2: God said,

4: Go and assemble the elders of Israel, and say to them, "The Lord, the God of your ancestors, the God of Abraham and Sarah, Isaac and Rebekah, and Jacob and Rachel has appeared to me, saying: 'I have given heed to you and to what has been done to you in Egypt. I will bring you up out of the misery of Egypt, to the land of the Canaanites, the Hittites, and the other tribes, a land flowing with milk and honey.'"

3: I am supposed to declare something? People like me don't declare anything, God.

4: They *will* listen to your voice. You and the elders of Israel shall go to the king of Egypt and say to him, "The Lord, the God of the Hebrews, has met with us; let us now go three days' journey into the wilderness so that we may sacrifice to the Lord our God." I know, however, that the king of Egypt will not let you go unless he is compelled by a mighty hand. So I will stretch out my hand and strike Egypt with wonders after that he will let you go.

3: You have got to be kidding me. Can I think about it?

SESSION 3
AWARENESS
UNDERSTANDING CULTURE

GOAL

Make the team aware of how culture affects one's life.

OBJECTIVES

- Discuss the team's culture.
- Provide a biblical basis for appreciating the value of other cultures.
- Establish principles for learning about culture.

SCRIPTURE TEXT

Exodus 1:8—2:15

PREPARATION

SUPPLIES ✓

- ❑ Flip chart or white board with markers
- ❑ Copies of the Psalm 146 handout, one per person (page 28)
- ❑ Extra copies of the journals, pens or pencils
- ❑ A Bible for each participant
- ❑ A copy of the Moses monologue, "Bridge Across Cultures" (page 29)
- ❑ Demographic information about both your trip destination and your own community (Responding 1)
- ❑ Materials to display this information: poster board, markers, old magazines, and scissors, glue, colored markers
- ❑ Copies of *Hymnal: A Worship Book* or song sheets

Tasks ✓

- ☐ Copy Psalm 146 for each participant.
- ☐ Invite a lay leader in your congregation to prepare the monologue, "Bridge Across Cultures" (page 29).
- ☐ For Responding to the Story, determine if you can do both activities in your time frame. This will have a bearing on the tasks below.
- ☐ For Activity 1 of Responding, gather information to give to groups to research their home area and destination.(Chambers of commerce, Wikipedia, or tourism bureaus are good sources for this information. The organization hosting you may also help.) Write the questions on the flip chart or board, leaving space to record answers.
- ☐ For Activity 2 of Responding, invite one or two congregational members who have worked cross culturally to join you and talk about the cultural shifts they experienced, and what these did for their appreciation of other cultures. Ask them to suggest a song or two from the other culture(s) to sing with the group. Otherwise, the following are some suggested titles from *Hymnal: A Worship Book*: 422, "Bwana Awabariki"; 537, "En Medio de la Vida"; 554, "Our Father Who Art in Heaven"; 575, "Precious Lord, Take My Hand".

Session

Opening (5 minutes)
Hand out copies of Psalm 146. Explain that there is an invitation for everyone to add their own declarations to the psalm.

Pray the psalm together.

Focusing (5 minutes)
Ask participants to think of one family tradition they follow for Christmas. Think of traditions around food, songs, decorations, or other customs.

After a few moments, form into groups of three to compare their answers. Each person should note which customs would feel strange to them, which ones would feel uncomfortable, and which ones would be refreshing additions to their own traditions.

Telling the biblical story (5 minutes)
Say: *Being at someone else's holiday traditions can make us aware of our own family culture. Moses was a bi-cultural person, growing up Egyptian while having Hebrew roots. Imagine what it would have been like to be in his role as a leader.*

Ask the group to turn to Exodus 1:8—2:15 in their Bibles. Have them read it silently or ask volunteers to read the text from the Bible.

Exploring the story (15 minutes)
Ask your guest reader to present the monologue, "Bridge Across Cultures."

Discuss:
- Why does Pharaoh ask the midwives to kill the Hebrew boy newborns?
- Why do you think Pharaoh's daughter rescued a Hebrew baby?
- How do you imagine Moses' childhood? Do you think he knew he was Hebrew?
- When Moses thinks, "Surely the thing is known." What is "the thing"?

EXTENDER ACTIVITY (PAGE 27)

When talking about serving cross culturally, it is important to have an open discussion about racism and white privilege—especially if you belong to the dominant white culture. For this, an extender activity following this session is recommended. It's best if you can take an extra session to do the activity, or else take time after this session.

Ask the students to turn in their journals to the questions for this session (journal page 5). Have them spend a few moments writing in their journals. Explain that group journaling is something they will do on the coming trip. The exercise also gives an opportunity for any students who have not started journaling to get on board with the activity.

If anyone has forgotten their journal, make paper available and encourage them to transfer their answers to their journal later.

RESPONDING TO THE STORY (20 MINUTES, EACH ACTIVITY)

Both of the following activities are great assets for your trip preparation. However, if your time allotment is an hour or less, you may need to choose the one that you think your group needs the most. Consider doing the other one as a separate session, possibly together with the extender activity on page 27.

After the activities, take time to review the team covenant, taking into account what they have learned about differences of culture and about serving across cultural borders.

1. Where are we going? Where are we now?

In this activity your group will gain understanding of cultural similarities and differences by comparing your own community to that of your service trip destination.

> Set out the literature and information about your community and the trip destination. Then say: *Moses was conscious of living and moving between two distinct cultures: his parents' Hebrew culture, and his adoptive Egyptian culture. We, too, will be crossing boundaries between cultures as we move from our own familiar community to the destination, where some things could be quite different.*

Divide into two groups. One group will study your home community; the other will study the community of your trip destination. Each group must find answers to the following questions and present them creatively on a poster, along with other interesting facts.

1. How many people live in the town, city, or area?
2. What is the ethnic make-up?
3. What options are available for local transportation?
4. What mode do most people use?
5. What are some of the main businesses or employers of the area?
6. What foods is the area known for?
7. Complete the sentence "If I were a tourist here, _____ would be a must-see attraction because."
8. What are three things that residents here would be known for? [numbered on the chart]
9. Give two interesting factoids (characteristics that may or may not be true) about this place. [numbered on the chart]

Ask each group to present what they found. Then use these questions for discussion:
- What are you surprised to learn about your home area?
- What are you surprised to learn about the trip destination?
- How are the areas similar?
- How are they different?
- How do the tourism books describe your home town? Is this an accurate picture?
- Do you believe that the tourism books give an accurate picture of where you are going?
- If someone who was reading your description of your home area had never been there, would they view your area as good, bad, or something else?
- If someone who was reading your description of your destination had never been there, would they view the area as good, bad, or something else?

Process these questions, and then attach the posters to the wall as reminders of the links between your own environment and that of your trip destination.

2. Guest speakers
If you haven't done the first activity, introduce this one with similar words to those used above in describing Moses.

Invite your visitors to speak for a few minutes about their experiences in another culture. Allow ample time for questions. Try to steer the discussion toward surprises, adjustments, and changes of cultural orientation that they had to experience. Nudge your youth to think critically about assumptions about their own culture (e.g. that it is better, or that it has nothing to learn from others.)

CLOSING (5 MINUTES)
Singing

Pass out hymnals and/or song sheets and sing songs you have chosen or the ones suggested by the guests.

PREPARATION FOR NEXT TIME:
Remind the group of the journal pages. Encourage them to take time to write additional thoughts and keep them for reference.

CULTURE HUNT

The following activity makes particular sense for youth groups who have not thought much about racism before and who are predominantly white. It is based on Peggy McIntosh's article entitled "White Privilege: Unpacking the Invisible Knapsack" (http://www.powervote.org/files/White%20Privilege.pdf), which can be a good way to start a conversation about racism. You may wish to summarize the article before the activity, or simply present the activity as a way to grapple with the issue of white privilege.

OBJECTIVE
See culture and white privilege as something that affects daily life.

LOCATIONS
A department store or mall, and a place to process the event.

MATERIALS
A copy of the "list of items" (below) and a digital camera for each team.

SET UP
1. This activity takes place in a mall or department store. If you are using a store, ask the manager ahead of time for permission to take pictures (see below). If you are using a mall, have each team ask permission at each store they visit (they can indicate they are doing a youth group project).
2. Split the group into teams of three or four, and give them each a list of items.
3. Ask each group to find each item on the list and to take a picture of it.
4. Establish an end time and place to meet at the end of the activity, then send the groups out.
5. Depending where you are, the list may not be completed. The point of the activity is to have youth realize that white privilege means having access to "normal" things that reflect our own culture. People of color do not have similar access.

LIST OF ITEMS
1. A Mariachi (a kind of Mexican) or an Aboriginal/Native American album
2. A greeting card that has people of color on it.
3. A "flesh-colored" band-aid for a person of color
4. A flag from another country
5. A picture book about a person of color

DISCUSSION
- What did you find? What did you not find?
- What surprised you as you did this hunt?
- If you are white, was it easier to find music from your point of view, a greeting card with white people, "flesh" band-aids, and a flag from the U.S. or Canada?
- What did you learn from this hunt?

What do you think this exercise has to do with issues of race and racism?

ALL: (*shouting like we mean it*)
Praise the Lord! Praise the Lord, O My Soul!

ALL: (*quietly, as if praying a prayer that only God can hear*)
I will praise the Lord as long as I live; I will sing praises to my God all my life long.

ADULT(S): Do not put your trust in princes, in mortals, in whom there is no help. When their breath departs, they return to the earth; on that very day their plans perish.

FEMALES: Happy are those whose help is from the God of Jacob, whose hope is in the Lord their God, who made heaven and earth, the sea, and all that is in them.

MALES: Who keeps faith forever; who executes justice for the oppressed; who gives food to the hungry.

ALL: (*with emphasis*)
The LORD sets prisoners free.

The LORD opens the eyes of the blind.

The LORD lifts up those who are bowed down.

The LORD loves the righteous.

The LORD watches over the strangers; he upholds the orphan and the widow, but the way of the wicked he brings to ruin.

LEADER: What else can we say about the LORD today from our own experiences? Say them out loud at this time.
(*Leave a few moments for spontaneous additions.*)

LEADER: The LORD will reign forever, your God, O Zion, for all generations. Praise the Lord.

ALL: Amen.

BRIDGE ACROSS CULTURES
MOSES' MONOLOGUE

I can understand both sides. You might not believe me, but really, I understand both sides.

Let me explain. In one sense, I am both Hebrew and Egyptian; and in another sense, I am neither Hebrew nor Egyptian.

I was born to a Hebrew woman in a time when Hebrews were slaves of the Egyptians. When I was a baby, the Pharaoh ordered that all boys born to Hebrew women were to be killed. To try to get around that edict, my mother placed me in a floating basket and sent me down the Nile River. I was rescued by another woman, my second mother—Pharaoh's daughter, who eventually adopted me. So I was raised as Egyptian royalty, got an education. Much was expected of me.

One day, when I was out on business among the slaves, my people, I saw a commander kill one of the slaves. I got mad and killed the commander. I skipped the country in fear of my life. In exile, I met my wife Zipporah and settled into a new life.

So, when I received the burning bush message to go stick it to Pharaoh, I wasn't at all excited. I wasn't at all pleased either when I realized that it wasn't the Hebrew people asking for my help—it was God. I wasn't raised by my Hebrew parents, so it didn't seem like they were really family; how could I speak on behalf of the Hebrews? Not to mention that to do so would be like speaking against the family I did know: the Egyptians. I might have been on the run, but the Egyptians were still the family I had.

I never really felt like an Egyptian. Nor did I feel at home in my Hebrew skin. Maybe that's why I could understand why the people should be let go, and also why it was so hard for Pharaoh to let them go. God's justice was at hand for the Hebrews, true. But the entire empire was built around the need for slave labor; if Pharaoh let me take my people to the Promised Land, his whole way of life would drastically change.

I crossed cultures daily within myself, and that helped me communicate. I knew the rituals of Hebrew life. I could understand; but it took work. I didn't learn my Hebrew culture in a day—Miriam and Aaron would often laugh when I would first say things like "Ah, in Egypt, we don't eat this . . ." And when I went back to Egypt, the Pharaoh shuddered when I said, "My people need compassion."

Learning cultures isn't easy—but it is possible. You are bound to encounter such different cultures, and I hope that you can start being a bridge, like I was.

SESSION 4
GOD'S ACTIVITY
JOINING IN GOD'S MISSION

GOAL

Develop in the team a solid understanding of God's reconciling work in the world, both in their home community and elsewhere.

OBJECTIVES

- Stimulate the team's thinking about how to be open to seeing the work of God.
- Provide a biblical basis for recognizing how God works in both ordinary and extraordinary ways.

SCRIPTURE TEXT

Exodus 15:22-27

PREPARATION

SUPPLIES ✓

- ❑ Flip chart or white board with markers
- ❑ One piece of poster or chart paper and several markers for each team of three people
- ❑ Three skeins of embroidery floss in three different colors, several scissors
- ❑ A copy of the readers theatre "Listen Up" for each participant (page 35)
- ❑ The team's theme song on paper or CD.
- ❑ Copies of a list of items each person should bring on the trip.
- ❑ Index cards and pencils (Responding)

Tasks ✓

- ☐ Ask three group members to perform the reader's theatre "Listen Up," and arrange a time to rehearse it.
- ☐ Invite to your session a person from your congregation who has a clear missional sense of God's calling in their lives—that is, they understand their work to be a joining with God in God's work. This person should not necessarily be in full-time ministry; in fact, they should model God's work in the world through typical lines of work that the youth can identify with. Give them your interview questions ahead of time: (see "Responding").
- ☐ Determine if you can do the extender activity (page 34) focusing on the discipline of silence. If so, plan what venue to use.
- ☐ Compile a packing list, weather information, etc., to hand out to your team. Your hosts will be your main source of this information.
- ☐ Cut embroidery floss into 18-inch/45-cm lengths, enough for each person to have one of each color.

Session

Opening (2 minutes)

Begin your session with a prayer: *Guiding God, you have gathered us to learn, serve and grow in this time. You also are already working in* (trip destination). *We thank you for those who participating in your work there. As we prepare to visit them, help us to find joy with you in their service, in their dedication, in their understandings of you. Help us prepare to see your miracles, your reconciling power, and your way in* (trip destination). *Amen.*

Focusing (5 minutes)

Give each person three strands of floss—one of each of the three colors. Explain that Color 1 represents oneself, Color 2 other people, and Color 3 God. Each strand has strength, but when braided together the three strands create something new without giving up their own identity.

Ask the youth to braid the strands together. (You may need to help those who have not braided before.) Knot the three strands together at one end and attach the end to a safety pin. To keep the threads taunt, attach the pin to jeans just above the knee. When the braid is complete, tie a knot at the other end. Set the bracelet aside until the closing time.

Telling the biblical story (5 minutes)

Hand out copies of "Listen Up," so that each person has a copy of the Scripture text for their reference. Have three readers present the text.

EXPLORING THE STORY (10 MINUTES)

Discuss the following questions:

- What do the Israelites expect of God in this story?
- What is given to them?
- Just prior to this story, we read about God's release of the Hebrews from slavery in Egypt, and the amazing parting of the Red Sea. [Review the story if it is not familiar to some.] Now, in today's story, what feelings may be swirling around within the Israelites?
- What role does the newly sweetened water play in the story?
- Why do you think God asked Moses to throw a stick in the water?
- How do you think Moses knew what to do to serve God's mission?
- Did God need Moses' cooperation for the water to turn from bitter to sweet?
- What is the test referred to in the reading? How was this a test?
- How is God a healing God?

Adapt the following thoughts in a mini-talk:

Back in Exodus 3 and Session 2, we read about Moses being called to join God's work with the Hebrew people. Moses walked in God's way throughout the story with his team of supporters. We can imagine Miriam, Moses, Aaron, and Zipporah, fresh from leading the Hebrew people out of slavery and through the Red, celebrating God's mighty act of deliverance. But now, there is no water.

Now what? God taps Moses to make the local water drinkable, and then leads the people to a place that has enough water for all the people. But consider God's words during the miracle of water: "If you will listen carefully, and do what is right, I will . . ." Yes God will heal them and will provide for them.

But God is asking for more. Moses listens to God and by doing so is able to collaborate with God's liberating work. Earlier, Moses listened and went to Egypt. Moses listened and led the people across the Red Sea. Now, Moses listens and acts as God makes bitter water drinkable.

God is asking for the people's patience and persistence in looking for ways to join God's work.

As you prepare to participate with God's workers in (destination of trip), may you look for ways that your hosts are connecting to God's kingdom and work. Ask: where is God working that you would never have guessed? Look for ways that your passion and God's passion can combine as you work. Listen to God to know where to join in the action.

RESPONDING TO THE STORY (30-35 MINUTES)

The two activities for this section are meant to help your group recognize that God's activity is everywhere, including here at home. Our task is to listen and look for signs and sightings of God's work in our world. How can we be aware and attentive to recognize the signs? How can we make ourselves ready to partner with God in fulfilling God's plans?

If your time is tight and you have to choose one activity, or you want to spend more time at one, determine which one best reflects the needs and character of the group. The second activity should be used if participants tend to think that God's work is "in a distant land," that is, some far-off location, and not at home.

ACTIVITY 1: GUEST SPEAKER (10 MINUTES)

Introduce your speaker, inviting her/him to talk briefly about their work. Use the following questions in an interview:

- What signs of God's activity do you see in the work you are doing?
- How are you working in partnership with God?
- How do you listen for God?
- How do you know what God wants to be done?
- What are the things you cry over?
- What are the things that you celebrate?
- What counsel can you give youth about partnering with God in God's mission in (destination) and (home)?

ACTIVITY 2: WHERE ARE WE SEEING THE ACTIVITY OF GOD? (20-25 MINUTES)

Divide the group into teams of three. Give each team a large sheet of paper and markers. Choose a member to jot down notes. Ask each team to reflect on the work of God, using the following questions:

- Where is the work of God clearly happening in our neighborhood, town, area?
- Where do we see ambiguity—where we can't tell whether or not God is at work?
- Is it easier to see signs of God's work in our own community or at a distance? Explain.
- How is our youth group joining in God's work here and now?
- How will the service we plan to do be part of God's work?
- What obstacles may we encounter when you look for God's work? How can they be removed?
- What joys (sweetness) do we anticipate when we are on our service trip?

After 10 minutes, gather as a large group and have each team report on their discussion. What common themes are noted? What ideas can you flag for local service in your community? Take a few moments to review the team covenant to see what might need to be added or changed, based on what the group has learned today. Record the changes and announce that you will prepare copies of the covenant for your actual trip.

Option (especially if you do *not* do the extender activity)

For the discussion of the questions above, post the questions on chart paper or white board. Read them together. Hand out pencils and index cards. Have the youth sit in silence for five minutes and reflect on these questions. Ask them to jot down notes as they listen for God's ideas in the quiet time. Then gather for large group sharing and record their thoughts on chart paper. Following this, do your review of the team covenant.

CLOSING (5 MINUTES)

Help each other put on the bracelets they made earlier. Tie the ends together, cutting to size if necessary.

Then gather in a circle. Have everyone extend their braceleted hand into the middle of the circle and lead them in a prayer:

> *Moving God, thank you for making your work so evident in our lives and those of those around us. Help us listen to you for more ways to connect to your work. May we never fall into just seeing you as a provider of our needs. Instead, help us see your vision and moving ever closer to your ways of being in your world.*

Sing or play your theme song.

PREPARATION FOR NEXT TIME:

Hand out information for the trip, such as packing lists and weather forecast, etc. Remind everyone that they will be asked to bring extra photos and their journals to the next session after returning home.

EXTENDER ACTIVITY

SPIRITUAL DISCIPLINE OF SILENCE (30 MINUTES)

Take participants to a public space in your area, such as a park or a mall. Give them 30 minutes to be silent. Even though there will be noise around them, their assignment is to listen to God within the activity of the world. They can use this time to meditate on God in whatever way they choose; they may walk, sit, kneel, or lie down. Encourage them to imagine God or Jesus beside them. What would they talk about? They may ponder the following questions (you could have copies ready, or have youth write them in their journals):

- What are signs that God is here?
- How can you partner with God in your daily life? What can you do to bring God's 'sweetness' to someone?
- What is God whispering to you about using your interests and gifts?
- Is God asking you to do something? What? Listen to your heart.
- What is God bringing to your mind that surprises you?

Following the silent time, give the group opportunity to share in pairs about the experience.

- What did you notice about being intentionally quiet?
- Where did you see God?
- How might you act on God's nudges?

From Exodus 15:22-27

1:   Then Moses ordered Israel to set out from the Red Sea, and they went into the wilderness of Shur. They went three days in the wilderness and found no water.

2:   But when they came to Marah, they could not drink the water of Marah because it was bitter. And the people complained against Moses, saying,

1,3: What shall we drink?

1:   Moses cried out to the Lord; and the Lord showed him a piece of wood; he threw it into the water, and the water became sweet. There the Lord made for them a statute and an ordinance and there he put them to the test. God said,

3:   If you will listen carefully to the voice of the Lord your God, and do what is right in his sight, and give heed to his commandments and keep all his statutes, I will not bring upon you any of the diseases that I brought upon the Egyptians; for I am the Lord who heals you.

2:   Then they came to Elim, where there were twelve springs of water and seventy palm trees; and they camped there by the water.

SESSION 5
FAITH IN ACTION
SERVING AND LEARNING
AWAY FROM HOME

GOAL

Experience God with your team as you serve and learn in an unfamiliar setting.

OBJECTIVES

- Offer your team opportunities to reflect on new experiences and perspectives.
- Provide biblical input that helps youth understand their experience.

PREPARATION

SUPPLIES TO COLLECT BEFORE DEPARTURE ✓

- ❏ copies of the team covenant (debriefing, Day 3)
- ❏ mailing address labels and stamps (debriefing, Day 4),
- ❏ paper and pens or pencils for group exercises

SUPPLIES TO COLLECT AFTER ARRIVAL ✓

- ❏ postcards (debriefing, Day 4)
- ❏ local bread for Bread of Life activity (debriefing, Day 5)

TASKS BEFORE DEPARTURE: ✓

- ❏ Collect addresses of home of supporters. This will include the Jethros, the financial supporters, any speakers who have come to your sessions, Sunday school teachers, and whomever else the group counts as supporters.
- ❏ Photocopy the team covenant, and determine when to hand them out (either at departure, or on arrival).
- ❏ Decide which of the activities below you will do and plan when and how you will obtain the supplies for them.

SESSIONS—GROUP PROCESSING AT THE END OF EACH DAY

Since this "session" is the service-learning experience itself, the following are guidelines for daily time you will spend together in debriefing. The guidelines are for two main components: (1) a time of Scripture reading and journaling, and (2) a reflective activity. Depending on your circumstances, you will decide how much of this material you are able to use.

If you are using a service-learning agency to plan the details of your stay, it may include guided reflection times in its program. If so, you may or may not have the time to do both of the components offered here. Give first priority to your host agency's plans. If possible, at least try to read the Scripture text together and, together or individually, the journaling. Also, since Sessions 6 depends on it, try to arrange some time for the Action Plans activity for Day 6.

If you have planned your own trip, the following will provide a continuation of what the previous sessions have been building on. The guide below is structured so that the Bible reading and journaling time is followed by the reflection activity.

In addition to the activities listed, consider singing your theme song and/or reviewing your team covenant each day.

■ DAY 1
Text: Exodus 15:1-4

1. Journaling
As a group, take at least 10 minutes to answer the journal questions for the day.

2. Quotes to match the day
Announce that you will read a few quotes from famous people. After each one, you will leave a few moments of silence to reflect on two questions:
- How do these quotes connect with what you experienced today?
- Do they agree with your day, or disagree with your day?

Be the change you wish to see in the world.
— Mohandas K. Gandhi

The ultimate measure of a person is not where he or she stands in the moments of comfort and convenience, but where she or he stands in times of challenge and controversy.
—Martin Luther King Jr.

You had to decide: Am I going to change the world, or am I going to change me? Or maybe change the world a little bit, just by changing me?
—Sadie Delany

As a Christian, I cannot not care about the environment, about homelessness and poverty, about racism and religious persecution, about justice and violence. God doesn't give me that option.
—Philip Yancey

Never doubt that a small group of thoughtful, committed people can change the world. Indeed, it is the only thing that ever has.
—Margaret Mead

Tell the group, if you haven't already, that for the first session following the trip, they will be asked to bring mementos, their journals, and extra pictures to help reflect upon the trip. They should already be thinking about what they will bring back. .

■ Day 2

Text: Exodus 19:1-7

1. Journaling

As a group, take at least 10 minutes to answer the journal questions for the day.

2. Intercession

Pray together for the people in the location you are serving. Have each participant pick a person or place that they have met or observed—someone whom they see as joining in God's mission. Celebrate their work in prayer.

■ Day 3

Text: Exodus 20:1-17

1. Journaling

As a group, take at least 10 minutes to answer the journal questions for the day.

2. Review of the team covenant

Distribute copies of your team covenant and read it together out loud. Then discuss the following questions:

- How well is our team upholding our covenant?
- How is the team covenant helping the team?
- Which points need special attention?
- How can we be more mindful of our commitment to each other?

If the conversation leads to a discussion of conflict within the group, be honest in this time. This could be a longer session, but try to make time for it.

■ Day 4

Text: Exodus 40

1. Journaling

As a group, take at least 10 minutes to answer the journal questions for the day.

2. Postcards for home

Write postcards to supporters back home. Have everyone write at least three on behalf of the team. The following questions can help get you started on the content.

- What did you do today?
- What has been your highlight so far?
- What do you want to remember when you get home?

■ Day 5

Text: Exodus 16:1-5

1. Journaling

As a group, take at least 10 minutes to answer the journal questions for the day.

2. Bread of Life reflection time

Set your local bread on a table in the middle of your meeting place. Then, if music is available, begin with a song, such as "I Am the Bread of Life"(*HWB* 472). Then say:
In our sessions we have been journaling with the Israelites through the wilderness. During that time, God provided the people with manna, life-sustaining bread. In John 6, Jesus talks about himself as the symbol of manna:

Then Jesus said to them, 'Very truly, I tell you, it was not Moses who gave you the bread from heaven, but it is my Father who gives you the true bread from heaven. For the bread of God is that which comes down from heaven and gives life to the world.' They said to him, 'Sir, give us this bread always.' Jesus said to them, 'I am the bread of life. Whoever comes to me will never be hungry, and whoever believes in me will never be thirsty.'" (John 6:32-35)

Jesus is life sustaining bread. Let's share this bread as a reminder of that life sustaining power that we have seen this week.

Pass the bread around and encourage each person to take a generous hunk. As they eat, if the group is comfortable doing so, have volunteers share one or two ways they have seen God's work (manna) or Jesus' power (bread of life) in action during this trip.

After all have eaten and/or shared, pray together: *Life-giving God, we are thankful for this trip and for all the ways you are working in the world. May this time be as yeast is to bread to us, prodding us to grow in order to share your work with others. Amen.*

■ DAY 6
Text: Joshua 1:1-9

1. Journaling
As a group, take at least 10 minutes to answer the journal questions for the day.

2. One word
Ask the group, *Have you ever asked someone "How are you?" expecting a one-word answer? Many people will ask about your trip, expecting a one word answer—not because they don't care but because it is what they expect. So, I want you to come up with one word to describe your trip—but it can't be sweet, cool, awesome, fine, good, or crappy. Find another word to describe it.* Give the group some time to reflect on their words, and then take turns sharing the word with the rest.

3. Action goals
This assignment will be revisited during next session, after your return home. But for now, come up with several action goals that emerge for you out of your experience—goals that you will continue to process and act upon after the trip. These will be a key part of you response to what you have experienced.

If the group is large, break into smaller groups of three or four (or divide into subgroups that you may have had on this trip), and have each group come up with at least one goal. Encourage them to let their imaginations roam free. The goal can be as ambitious as starting a non-profit agency, or it could be as practical as reporting back to your congregation about what you have learned. After each group has settled on a goal, they should begin jotting thoughts about the following:
- What is needed to accomplish that goal? (e.g. serving Thanksgiving dinner in a homeless shelter in your home community)
- What are three specific steps that flow out of that goal? (e.g. contact the shelter; book a time for the project; and invite another youth group to join you.)

Both in the smaller groups and in the large-group sharing afterward, write down your goals and steps and keep these for reference in Sessions 6 and 7.

Important: Remind the youth to bring their mementos, their journals, and extra pictures to the next session, which will involve a lot of reflection and processing of the trip.

REFLECTION
WHAT DID WE JUST DO?

GOAL

Provide the team with tools for reflection on their experience so that they can use that experience in moving into future action and reflection.

OBJECTIVES

- Debrief on the trip experience.
- Offer a biblical basis for the team's readjustment to life at home.

SCRIPTURE TEXT

Joshua 3:1-17

PREPARATION

SUPPLIES ✓

- ❑ Flip chart or white board with markers
- ❑ Large container (such as a laundry basket) to use as an "ark" for objects that the team members bring (mementos, pictures, journals etc.)
- ❑ Three copies of the readers theatre, "Crossing over Jordan" (page 45)
- ❑ Materials to construct your "Jordan River" (a child's wading pool, or a strip of blue cloth)
- ❑ Scrapbook with removable pages—two pages per participant, and if your group had sub-groups, two pages per group, plus at least six pages for the group as a whole
- ❑ Markers, adhesive, and other scrapbooking material
- ❑ Notes from conversations about action goals (Session 5, day 6)
- ❑ Paper and pen for the note taker

Tasks ✓

❑ Remind youth to bring extra photos, mementos, and journals to session.

❑ Invite your "Jethros," parents, and others who were with you in spirit during the trip, to join you for the opening and the Scripture story.

❑ Assign two readers besides yourself for the readers theatre, and arrange a time to practice.

❑ Gather notes from your conversations during the trip, including the action goals discussion.

❑ Post the goals and action steps from Session 5 (Day 6).

❑ Copy the readers theatre, "Crossing over Jordan" (page 45).

❑ Think through venue possibilities for the Jordan River ceremony (see "Telling the biblical story").

❑ Think through your improvisations on the readers theatre.

Session

Opening (5 minutes)

As youth arrive, ask them to put their photos, mementos, and journals into your "ark." Reassure them that the journals will not be read, and the mementos and pictures will be used for the scrapbook you will create. The journals and any mementos they do not want to be shared will be returned.

Welcome your Jethros and any other visitors.

Focusing (5 minutes)

Gather in a circle around the ark and pray. Use the following as a model, incorporating experiences from your own trip.

Guiding God, You were with us in the blue van and in all the rest stops. You were with us when we arrived to find out the air conditioning was out. You were there when we heard the church choir's testimonies. You were there when we saw the homeless person who knew the Bible better than any of us. You were there when we met Daisy. You were there when we smelled the rain. You were there when we tasted the soul food that Arnie cooked for us. You were there, Lord, you were there.

And now? Now you are here, guiding God. We praise you for journeying with us wherever we are. Amen.

Telling the biblical story (15 minutes)

Explain that today's story comes at the end of Israel's 40 years in the desert. Moses is dead, and we're not sure who in his original team is still alive. But the team lives on in Joshua and the other leaders of the people; the journey is the same, even if the characters have changed.

Act out the story of Israel's crossing of the Jordan River, while also reflecting on your trip. Here are some options for your arrangements:

1. Gather outside the worship space, and use the threshold into it as the Jordan crossing.

2. Use a child sized wading pool or a strip of blue cloth to signify the river, and have your team step into it and walk to the other side.

The text for today is arranged in a choose-your-own-adventure style with three readers. As Reader 2, plan to improvise, since you will be asking the youth to place themselves in the story. If other questions seem more appropriate than the ones given, please ask those. Think through the possible answers for the questions that are included in the script, as well as for those that you are adding.

Begin with an introduction such as: *So now we are home. How do the people of Israel "come home"? How do they celebrate? Let's hear the story.*

Have your readers present the readers theatre. At the point where you and your team cross the river, have all your visitors form a line and offer a "welcome back" handshake to each person as they cross the "river."

EXPLORING THE STORY (10 MINUTES)
Discuss:
- Why do you think Joshua asked the Israelites to organize themselves before they crossed the Jordan?
- What is significant about the parting of the Jordan?
- Does this event end a larger story, or does it start a new one?
- What do you think of Joshua, rather than Moses, leading the people into the Promised Land?

Wrap up the discussion with the following summary:
The Hebrew people have had quite a journey. They were enslaved, then were released, spent a generation in the wilderness, and then finally are now led into the Promised Land. Moses has turned leadership over to Joshua.

While we haven't been on quite the same journey, we have experienced the story at different levels. Our team developed somewhat along the lines of the leadership team of Miriam, Moses, Aaron, and Zipporah. Like that team, we too had people back home who supported us—our Jethros. Like Moses, we found ways to meet God. Like the Exodus team, ours has taken seriously the call to cross cultural barriers. Our team has continued to look for ways to join God in God's mission of healing and hope. Our team has experienced the joys and struggles of being in an unfamiliar place. Now what?

Joshua is leading the people to a new home. We too will be experiencing a "new" home. We have returned home changed. Our home may look different to us, and our daily lives might be different. Just as Joshua asked the people to prepare for the blessing of their new Promised Land, we will prepare for a new understanding of our home.

At the same time, it is important to celebrate the larger stories and traditions we find ourselves in. God parts the Jordan River not only to open the way to Israel's future, but to give the people a reminder of God's care and provision. The parting of the waters of the Jordan reminds the people of the parting of the Red Sea. They know they are continuing a long journey with God—past, present and future. And it's the same with us. We remember and we celebrate, even as we move into God's future.

Responding to the story (30 - 35 minutes)
1. Memory Scrapbook (20 minutes)

This project will be started in this session, but unless you have at least another hour, it will probably need to be completed at another point. So consider organizing how that will happen. You may consider "commissioning" one member (perhaps a seasoned scrapbooker) to complete the team pages after this session is over.

The suggested format for the book is as follows:
- 2 pages for each person: mementos, photos, quotes from journal entries, captions
- 2 pages for each sub-group (if you had sub-groups), each highlighting the activities of the group
- 6 pages for the entire group: quotes, lyrics of the group song, team covenant, and group pictures with captions

Introduce the activity and explain the format for the book. Take a few minutes for work on individual pages, then work on the group pages together. Attach pictures, captions, documents you picked up—anything you feel will create a meaningful record for yourselves and for your congregation. If you have avid scrapbookers in your group, draw on their expertise.

Option A

Either preceding your scrapbook activity or instead of it, simply have a time of sharing your best memories—especially if you haven't had opportunity to do so in previous sessions or on the trip home. Have the youth turn to their journal pages and share items from what they wrote during the trip—particularly from Day 5. Other questions that may help them review could include the following in a "prayer of examen" exercise:
- What were the highlights of the trip? What were the "aha" moments for you?
- What made you sad in what you observed, how you behaved, what others did?
- Where did you sense God's guiding hand or feel God's presence in a special way?
- What is the good news that you received?
- What is the good news that you shared with others? Give an example.

Option B

If your group is technologically inclined, consider planning a Powerpoint presentation for your congregation instead of, or in addition to, a scrapbook.

From your "ark" select which pictures, captions, stories you will use to capture the essence of the service trip that will inspire and inform the congregation.

2. Action Goals (10 - 15 minutes)

Explain that part of your memories of the trip include the action goals you decided on in Session 5. To keep the momentum rolling, review them briefly now, and work on them further in Session 7.

Post the goals from Session 5 (Day 6 reflection time) where all can see them, and have participants take turns reading them out loud. Ask your note taker to record the main points of the following conversation.

For each goal ask:
1. Why did we choose this goal? What experience influenced us?
2. What further information do we need before we start implementing the goal?
3. Who will gather the information?

Example 1

If the goal was "Give a presentation to the congregation on our experiences" the fact finders should find a date in the church calendar where this would be a good fit. Session 7 might include a planning session for this presentation.

Example 2

If the goal was "Find out what are the needs of the homeless population in our town" your group may need to go deeper in their research, probably with your assistance. Before Session 7, the fact finders could do some initial calls or online research (e.g., what homeless shelters exist in the city). Then in Session 7, the group would determine what to do with the information (e.g., plan a visit to one of the shelters).

Ask your volunteer fact finders to stay for a few moments after the session to work out what needs to be done before next session.

Note: *Be sure to keep these action step plans and notes for next session. As the leader you may need to work with your youth, learning alongside them as they begin to follow up on the steps.*

CLOSING (5 MINUTES)

Gather your thanks and petitions from your memories of your trip. Stand in a circle and introduce the prayer like this:

> *To close our time of celebration, we will give thanks for people and events of the trip for which we feel especially blessed—and we will pray for people and situations for whom we are concerned-. We will have two rounds of sentence prayers, where each of us can name one or more item. After each item, we will respond in unison. For the thanksgiving items, we will all say, "Thank you, God." For the prayer items, we will say, "God, hear our prayer." (Example: "For the wonderful meals that John Doe cooked for us . . . Thank you, God.")*

> *I will start the prayer, and when I am finished with my items, I will squeeze the hand of the person to the right of me. He or she will do speak their items (again, with a group response after each one), and then squeeze the hand of the next person. Those who prefer not to share may immediately squeeze the hand of the next person. After the two rounds of thanksgiving and prayer, I will wrap up our time with a closing prayer.*

After the last person has prayed, gather everyone's sharing together in an integrated prayer of your own.

Sing or play theme your theme song.

CROSSING OVER JORDAN

Readers theatre based on Joshua 3:1-17

Note: the team leader will be Person 2

1: Early in the morning Joshua rose and set out from Shittim with all the Israelites, and they came to the Jordan. They camped there before crossing over. At the end of three days the officers went through the camp and commanded the people, "When you see the ark of the covenant of the Lord your God being carried by the levitical priests, then you shall set out from your place. Follow it, so that you may know the way you should go, for you have not passed this way before. Yet there shall be a space between you and it, a distance of about two thousand cubits; do not come any nearer to it." Then Joshua said to the people, "Sanctify yourselves; for tomorrow the Lord will do wonders among you." To the priests Joshua said, "Take up the ark of the covenant, and pass on in front of the people." So they took up the ark of the covenant and went in front of the people.

2: [*Improvise on the following.*] What would that look like for us? Let's see. Well, we have been traveling, we have camped out in [*place*] we have been home for [*number*] days. We have what we brought from our desert experience (*pick up container with the pictures, journals, etc*)—that is our ark. Who is Joshua? Who might be our priests? [*Participants pick their peers for these positions, who then walk in front of the rest of the group with the ark in the rest of the reading.*] Let's have them carry our ark and show it to the people.

1: The Lord said to Joshua, "This day I will begin to exalt you in the sight of all Israel, so that they may know that I will be with you as I was with Moses. You are the one who shall command the priests who bear the ark of the covenant, 'When you come to the edge of the waters of the Jordan, you shall stand still in the Jordan.'" Joshua then said to the Israelites,

3: "Draw near and hear the words of the Lord your God. By this you shall know that among you is the living God who without fail will drive out from before you the Canaanites, Hittites, Hivites, Perizzites, Girgashites, Amorites, and Jebusites: the ark of the covenant of the Lord of all the earth is going to pass before you into the Jordan. So now select twelve men from the tribes of Israel, one from each tribe. When the soles of the feet of the priests who bear the ark of the Lord, the Lord of all the earth, rest in the waters of the Jordan, the waters of the Jordan flowing from above shall be cut off; they shall stand in a single heap."

2: Who are our tribes? [*Divide your group into several smaller groups. If your service experience had already broken your group into sub-teams, use those groupings.*]

1: When the people set out from their tents to cross over the Jordan, the priests bearing the ark of the covenant were in front of the people. Now the Jordan overflows all its banks throughout the time of harvest. So when those who bore the ark had come to the Jordan, and the feet of the priests bearing the ark were dipped in the edge of the water, the waters flowing from above stood still, rising up in a single heap far off at Adam, the city that is beside Zarethan, while those flowing toward the sea of the Arabah, the Dead Sea, were wholly cut off. Then the people crossed over opposite Jericho. While all Israel were crossing over on dry ground, the priests who bore the ark of the covenant of the Lord stood on dry ground in the middle of the Jordan, until the entire nation finished crossing over the Jordan.

2: Let's cross over the Jordan. Priests, you go first and part the water with a wave of your hand, and then the rest of the group will walk through the dry river. Anything else we need to do? (*Youth may have other creative ways to insert themselves in the story.*)

At this point the whole group crosses over. Your visitors may form a line and offer a "welcome back" handshake to each person as they cross.

INTEGRATION
WHAT TO DO
WITH WHAT WE LEARNED

GOAL

Begin to integrate into daily living the lessons of the earlier experiences of preparation, service, and debriefing.

OBJECTIVES

- Celebrate God's work in our lives.
- Allow action goals to move toward action.
- Provide a biblical basis to continue a lifestyle of service

SCRIPTURE TEXT

Exodus 15:1-21

PREPARATION

SUPPLIES ✓

- ❑ Flip chart or white board and markers
- ❑ Copies of the Lord's Prayer for those who may not know it (*HWB* 731)
- ❑ Copies of the responsive reading (page 52)
- ❑ Floor space large enough for the focus activity
- ❑ Tambourines—one for every four people
- ❑ Permanent markers
- ❑ Colorful ribbons 12-18 inches long, one for each person and one for each group goal
- ❑ Copies of *Hymnal: A Worship Book*
- ❑ Scrapbook supplies from last week
- ❑ Snacks or a meal to follow the session

Consider how you will use or display the tambourines as a constant reminder of the action goals for the next six months to a year. If tambourines are used in your church worship, you might want to add these ones to the worship instruments. If not, the tambourines could be hung up on the wall in your meeting room. Throughout the coming year, choose a time during Sunday school and youth group to revisit the goals that are written on the ribbons. Ask the following questions: *How is God working in your life? Are you remembering what you learned? Are you making the changes that you wanted to make in your life?*

TASKS ✓

❑ Set up the flip chart for the group activity.

❑ Ask one person to be prepared to lead the responsive reading.

❑ Ask youth to bring their journals from the trip.

❑ Ask parents of the youth, your "Jethros," your pastor, and/or other congregational leaders to join you for this session. Ask one of them to lead the final responsive prayer.

❑ Find people to prepare and serve refreshments at the end of the session.

❑ Categorize the goals you have collected over the last two sessions, along with their action steps. (For example, if two goals have a recycling theme, gathering them into one might help your group better process them.) Post these goals and action steps in your meeting room.

❑ Make sure your meeting place has enough floor space for the focus activity.

SESSION

OPENING (5 MINUTES)

Read the Lord's Prayer together from your hymnals or recite it together. Then ask: How would you describe this prayer? Together, count how many action words the prayer contains, and allow comments on the kinds of verbs there are. Say: *This prayer is asking a lot, demanding justice each day from God.* Say the words again, this time as a prayer.

FOCUSING (5 MINUTES)

Ask the youth and any visitors who wish to do so, to do 10 sit-ups or 10 push-ups. Once everyone is done, ask: *When did you learn how to do sit up or push ups?* [Typical answers include—kindergarten, elementary school, really early.] *Were you ever tested on these? Do you like doing these exercises? Are they easy?* [Typical answers are: "No they are hard, I hate doing them." Some might say " I like the routine" or "I do them to warm up."]

Say: *Sit-ups and push-ups aren't always easy, but they are the building blocks for fitness. In the same way, acts of service can be building blocks for a lifelong commitment of faith. The learning you did through our service experience helps you get in the habit of putting put your faith into action.*

TELLING THE BIBLICAL STORY (5 MINUTES)

The Lord's Prayer demands justice, fitness demands excellence, and today's Scripture calls for a celebration of the justice and excellence of God. Our text today is the song that the Israelites sang just after they crossed the Red Sea after being liberated from slavery in Egypt. From this point, they will begin a new chapter of spiritual growth as God's people.

Hand out copies of the responsive reading and read through it.

EXPLORING THE STORY (15 MINUTES)

Discuss:

- What would this text have meant to the people of Israel, now that they had left slavery and Egypt behind and are now on the edge of an unknown wilderness?
- Why does so much of the song replay the past?
- Mull over the words, "In your steadfast love you led the people whom you redeemed; you guided them by your strength to your holy abode." How might this describe our lives, both as individuals, and as a group?

Offer the following thoughts in a mini-talk:

Miriam sings a song of joy declaring how God has worked in the Hebrew people after they are released from slavery. It is clear that living with God is at the heart of their life as a people. As we've seen in other sessions, the Red Sea experience is followed by the wilderness, where God's involvement with the people will sometimes be called into question. Sometimes after a trip like the one you experienced, it is easy to praise, easy to declare the important role of God. Then life happens. How will we live out the lessons we learned?

The story of the Israelites continues all through the Bible. Sometimes they were right on target with God's desires for them, and sometimes they missed the mark. Being a child of God involves the whole range of who we are; we're not perfect, but we are part of a journey where grace, compassion, love, and challenge are all found.

In our last session, we remembered our trip highlights—our "aha" moments, our personal learnings, and the dreams and goals that were born. Now, as we enter the "wilderness," we know that moving to a new place will always include challenges. We know it won't be easy—but we do know that God is there with us. We know what God has done and is doing—it is out of that hope that we continue finding our passion to join in God's mission, God's work in the world. Just as the Israelites allowed their celebration to energize them for their journey ahead, we will now think of how our celebration moves to action.

RESPONDING TO THE STORY (20 MINUTES)

1. Action goals (10 minutes)

Draw the group's attention to all the goals and action steps that you have categorized and posted on the wall. It is important to acknowledge each goal, even if you will not be able to treat each one in detail in this session. Have the group decide on which goals to work on during this session (likely ones which you began to work on last time). Have the fact finders (from Session 6) report on what they found out since last session.

The following questions will help further the conversation about next steps for each goal. In this session, you may only be able to address one or two goals. The others may require follow up in future sessions, or different action groups :

- Based on what the fact finders found, what are the next steps?
- Based on the new information, do we need change our plans?
- What other people beyond our group should be involved?
- What is our timeline?
- Who is responsible for what?
- What do we need to do today to work on these steps?

As leader, be flexible and ready for surprises. The action may not flow in the way that you might have chosen if you were directing this. Be careful to let the youth take ownership of the projects.

Example 1

If the action step was, "Give a presentation of our experiences to the congregation," the fact finders may have picked out a date in the church calendar where this would be a good fit. Instead of working through the list of given questions, it might be best to let the next few minutes become a planning session for how to present to the congregation. Other goals on your list may need to be attended to at a different time.

Example 2

If the action goal was "Determine what the needs of the homeless population in our home area are," this will not only take more planning than you can do in this session, but likely some education in figuring out how to go about this task.

Option

Sharing personal goals. It is possible that you would rather use this "respond" time to focus on personal, rather than group goals. (You have decided to have separate planning sessions to work further with your group goals, and/or you have not yet been able to have a good time of personal sharing.) If so, give opportunity for youth to gather in smaller groups to share, using the following questions and their own journals as a guide:

- How were my personal goals and expectations for the trip met? (see Session 1 journal)
- How can I imagine my life being different as a result of this trip? (Session 5 journal)
- Where in my life and in my community will I expect to see God at work?
- What specific acts of service will I be taking on as a result of this trip?
- What new habits of thoughts and action do I see taking root in my life?

Gather in a larger group and allow some time for sharing highlights.

2. Team Covenant (10 minutes)

If the team covenant was helpful to you for your trip, this activity can now help your group work with your goals and action steps. Have the group revisit the covenant and consider the value of a similar agreement for the future, while you implement your action steps Some of the covenant will directly transfer (such as "Respect each person's opinion"); other elements will not transfer (such as "Learn about Chicago"). But let the group grapple with what is now needed as you ask:

- What was the value of having a covenant?
- What might have been different if we did not have a covenant?
- Did we stick to the covenant?
- Could our existing covenant be carried forward for the future?
- If we need to revise it, based on our recent experience, what do we need to add?
- What would we wish to subtract or adapt?

Note: Unless you carry forward your existing covenant or your revisions are very straightforward, you may need to plan another session to work on the covenant.

Closing (20 minutes)
Celebration

Sing "Here in this place" (*HWB* 6) or another similar song.

> Say: *Exodus 15, song of Miriam, is a celebration of God's work. In Exodus 15:20 Miriam and all the women used tambourines to proclaim God's victory in the world. We are going to use tambourines to celebrate our trip and what we are committing to do.*

Ask everyone to take a ribbon and write on it their personal goals for the trip as indicated in their journals (Session 1)—as well as personal goals for service that may have formed during and after the trip. Also, ask for volunteers to write the group goals on ribbons, one goal per ribbon. When all the goals are written, tie the ribbons to the tambourines.

> Introduce the closing prayer (the second item in the handout) in this way: *We are going to pray a prayer of celebration. Your response will be, "We celebrate, and we will worship and serve our God!"* Ask them to repeat the response. *When we say, "celebrate," wave your hands or play the tambourines if you have one. When we say "worship," hold your palms up in the air. When we say "serve our God" shuffle your feet, walking on the spot.*

Lead the celebration prayer.

Invite all the parents, pastors, and supporters to a refreshment time afterwards.

Responsive Scripture reading based on Exodus 15:1-21

Leader: Then Miriam and the Israelites sang this song to the Lord:

All: I will sing to the Lord, for he has triumphed gloriously; horse and rider he has thrown into the sea. The Lord is my strength and my might, and he has become my salvation; this is my God, and I will praise him, my father's God, and I will exalt him. The Lord is a warrior; the Lord is his name.

Males: Pharaoh's chariots and his army he cast into the sea; his picked officers were sunk in the Red Sea. The floods covered them; they went down into the depths like a stone. Your right hand, O Lord, glorious in power—your right hand, O Lord, shattered the enemy.

Females: In the greatness of your majesty you overthrew your adversaries; you sent out your fury, it consumed them like stubble. At the blast of your nostrils the waters piled up, the floods stood up in a heap; the deeps congealed in the heart of the sea.

Leader: The enemy said, 'I will pursue, I will overtake, I will divide the spoil, my desire shall have its fill of them. I will draw my sword, my hand shall destroy them.'

Females: You, God, blew with your wind, the sea covered them; they sank like lead in the mighty waters.

Males: Who is like you, O Lord, among the gods?

Females: Who is like you, majestic in holiness, awesome in splendor, doing wonders? You stretched out your right hand, the earth swallowed them.

All: In your steadfast love you led the people whom you redeemed; you guided them by your strength to your holy abode.

Males: The peoples heard, they trembled; pangs seized the inhabitants of Philistia. Then the chiefs of Edom were dismayed; trembling seized the leaders of Moab; all the inhabitants of Canaan melted away. Terror and dread fell upon them; by the might of your arm, they became still as a stone until your people, O Lord, passed by, until the people whom you acquired passed by.

All: You brought them in and planted them on the mountain of your own possession, the place, O Lord, that you made your abode, the sanctuary, O Lord, that your hands have established. The Lord will reign forever and ever.

Females: When the horses of Pharaoh with his chariots and his chariot drivers went into the sea, the Lord brought back the waters of the sea upon them; but the Israelites walked through the sea on dry ground.

All: In your steadfast love you led the people whom you redeemed; you guided them by your strength to your holy abode.

Responsive Closing Prayer

Leader: We say together:

All: We celebrate. we will worship and serve our God!

Leader: We are here together; that is reason to celebrate.

We have worshipped together, and we will continue to worship God.

We have served God and we want to continue serving God, that is reason to celebrate.

We are here to be a witness to God's action in the world; that is reason to celebrate.

All: We celebrate, and we will worship and serve our God!

Leader: We are God's children ready to do God's work . . . World, here we come!

All: We celebrate, and we will worship and serve our God!

Leader: God is our God; who is worthy to be praised.

All: We celebrate, and we will worship and serve our God!

Instructions for *Merge Journal* assembly

Photocopy the *Merge Journal* pages, front to back, just as they appear here. There should be a total of five 8.5"x11" sheets for each journal you create.

Fold the pages down the middle and stack them according to the following diagram:

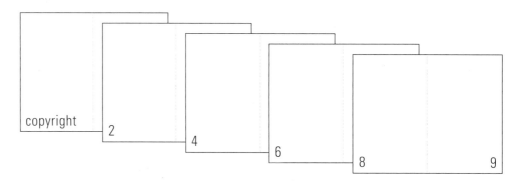

Staple the pages together at the "spine" of the journal.

*Tip: If you are using a regular office stapler, it can be hard to reach the spine. Try this for easier stapling: place the pages against a firm but penetrable surface, such as a bulletin or cork board. Open the stapler and place 2-3 staples through the spine and into the board. Remove the journal from the board and bend the staples into place.

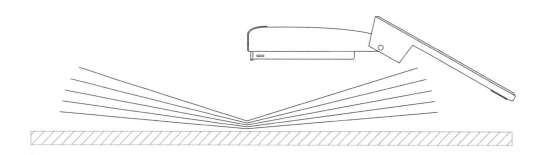

Merge may sound like a strange title for this book. But it was chosen deliberately, and not just because of all the "merge" signs you will see on the highways you travel when you go on your service trip. For Christian believers, a life of service is all about joining God's work in history. God is active in the world, healing, restoring, and bringing in God's *shalom* through Christ. God has brought light into our own lives. In response, we merge our wills and our energies with God's, allowing ourselves to be instruments of God's peace.

TRUST
BUILDING A TEAM

SCRIPTURE TEXT

Exodus 4:18-31

Why have I decided to go on this trip?

_____

_____

_____

These are my personal goals:

_____

_____

_____

What role might God want me to have in the group? (Am I most like Jethro, Moses, Zipporah, Aaron, or Miriam?)

_____

_____

What are three things I need to know about people before joining a team?

1. _____

2. _____

3. _____

What are three things people need to know about me?

1. _____

2. _____

3. _____

What is my working style:

☐ I work best under deadline pressures.

☐ I like lots of advance planning.

☐ I'm spontaneous.

☐ I'm more of an individual than team player.

In our group, the people most like the biblical characters are:

Jethro _____

Zipporah _____

Moses _____

Miriam _____

Aaron _____

MORE
JOURNAL NOTES

INNER LIFE
PREPARING TO MEET GOD

SCRIPTURE TEXT

Exodus 3:1-12

How would I describe my journey with God?

_____

_____

At the start of this trip, am I at a spiritual beginning? a highpoint in the middle? the end of a long preparation?

beginning   middle   end

Am I more prepared to "go to Egypt"? (see new places and things) or to see a "burning bush" (encounter God in new ways)? How?

_____

_____

INTEGRATION
WHAT TO DO WITH WHAT WE LEARNED

SCRIPTURE TEXT

Exodus 15:1-21

In Exodus 15, Miriam leads a celebration of God's mighty act of deliverance. In my living, how can I celebrate God's work in the world?

_____

_____

How am I getting involved in the action steps our group has chosen?

_____

_____

How do I want to be working on these action steps a month from now? Six months from now?

_____

_____

What has been my biggest lesson during this whole service trip experience?

_____

_____

REFLECTION
WHAT DID WE JUST DO?

SCRIPTURE TEXT

Joshua 3:1-17

Now that I am back from the service and learning trip, in what ways have I felt that I am in a "new" home?

What has felt strange since I came home?

What has felt comforting?

What effect do I want this trip to have six months from now? A year from now?

What excites me? What scares me?

Excites	Scares

When I picture myself arriving home from the trip, what do I imagine myself celebrating about it? What will I be sad about?

AWARENESS
UNDERSTANDING CULTURE

SCRIPTURE TEXT

Exodus 1:8-2:15

How is Moses a bridge builder?

When and where have I crossed cultural boundaries? What was confusing about the experience(s)? What was encouraging?

What do I imagine is Moses' hardest challenge in being a bridge between Egyptian and Israelite culture?

Do I currently live between two cultures? How does that feel?

SCRIPTURE TEXT

Joshua 1:1-9

The Israelites are going "home" to the Promised Land. We are winding down our time on this trip. May our return home be a time of comfort and challenge as we work through what we learned these last few days.

What lessons am I taking home with me?

What is the first thing I am going to do when I arrive home?

What am I worried about as I go home? How am I going to tackle that worry?

What personal challenges do I want to work on after this trip?

Reminder: Bring journal, mementos, and extra photos to the next session.

GOD'S ACTIVITY
JOINING IN GOD'S MISSION

SCRIPTURE TEXT

Exodus 15:22-27

In what ways am I connected to God's work?

God recognized the "groaning of the people" in enslavement (Exodus 2:23-25, Exodus 6:4-5). What is worth groaning over today? What can I do to help to turn my groaning into laughter?

What is God celebrating? How am I joining in the celebration?

THE TRIP

The wilderness isn't all that it is cracked up to be. The people of Israel complain that the food was better in Egypt, sometimes forgetting that God's gift of manna is keeping them alive on their journey. Service trips, too, come with challenges. May we find "manna"—God's sustaining nourishment to pull us through.

SCRIPTURE TEXT: EXODUS 16:1-5

What has been a struggle for me during this trip?

How is God working in me through the struggle?

What things have been "manna" to me?

What things surprise me about the "wilderness" of this trip?

FAITH IN ACTION
SERVING AND LEARNING AWAY FROM HOME

SCRIPTURE TEXT

Exodus 15:1-4

There is much to celebrate today! As Moses and the team are able to celebrate the end of slavery and the start of freedom, we are free to experience this new place. May we be in awe of what God is doing here!

Where have I seen God today?

What things are inspiring me?

What things are different from home?

What has made me smile?

What do I want to remember from today?

SCRIPTURE TEXT

Exodus 40

The Israelites construct a tabernacle—a temporary building that will serve as a place to meet God until a permanent temple is built. At the end of Exodus 40, we read how God fills the tabernacle with God's glory. May God's glory fill this trip!

Where did God's glory show up today?

Where did God's reign of love become evident to me?

How did I pass on God's grace to others?

SCRIPTURE TEXT

Exodus 19:1-7

Moses continues to meet God in the wilderness. During our service trip it may be easy to get so busy in God's work that we forget to take time to seek God. May we encounter God in very real ways on this trip.

Where did I meet God today?

_____
_____
_____

Who did I meet today who was God-filled?

_____
_____

What characteristics made them seem God-filled?

_____
_____

How do I see God working here?

_____
_____
_____

SCRIPTURE TEXT

Exodus 20:1-17

During the time in the wilderness, the Israelites are given rules to live by, a structure for their life as a community. The service team covenant is, in some ways, like the Ten Commandments. It is a tool to keep us focused on our call and commitment. May we find it helpful during these days.

How is the team covenant working for me? How is it easy to follow? How is it hard?

_____
_____

How am I adjusting to a new routine? Is it exciting or exhausting? Or both?

_____
_____

What do I admire among the people and programs I'm working with?

_____
_____

What do I miss about my routine at home?

_____
_____

SUGGESTED RESOURCES

TEAM BUILDING (SESSION 1)

Pollack, Stanley, and Mary Fusoni. *Moving Beyond Icebreakers: An Innovative Approach to Group Facilitation, Learning, and Action.* Danbury: Center for Teen Empowerment Incorporated, 2005.

For ideas for icebreakers, go to: http://www.group-games.com/category/ice-breakers

SPIRITUAL DISCIPLINES (SESSION 2)

Bass, Dorothy C. *Practicing Our Faith: A Way of Life for a Searching People.* San Francisco: Jossey-Bass, 1998.

Foster, Richard J. *Celebration of Discipline: The Path to Spiritual Growth.* New York: Harper San Francisco, 2003.

RACE AND CLASS ISSUES (SESSION 3)

Ehrenreich, Barbara. *Nickel and Dimed: On (Not) Getting by in America.* New York: St. Martin's Press, 2003.

Terkel, Studs. *Race: How Blacks and Whites Think and Feel about the American Obsession.* New York: New Press, 2005.

MISSIONAL CHURCH THINKING (SESSION 4)

The Missio Dei series of Mennonite Mission Network
mennonitemission.net/resources/Publications/MissioDei

Krabill, James R. *Does Your Church "Smell" Like Mission?* Missio Dei, Volume 2. Elkhart, Indiana: Mennonite Board of Missions, 2003.

Kraybill, James R., and Stuart W. Showalter, editors. *Students Talk about Service,* Missio Dei, Volume 7. Elkhart, Indiana: Mennonite Board of Missions, 2004.

Wyse, Jackie. James R. Kraybill, editor. *Digging for Treasure in Your Own Backyard,* Missio Dei, Volume 15. Elkhart, Indiana: Mennonite Board of Missions, 2007.

Web Links

Pathways to a Missional Future
http://www.mennoniteusa.org/Home/MissionalChurch/tabid/123/Default.aspx

Circles of Relationships
http://www.youtube.com/watch?v=IB4mdOckkjk

In This Time, In This Place: Five Missional Stories
http://store.mennomedia.org/p-219-in-this-time-in-this-place-five-missional-stories.aspx

I Traveled to Ireland
http://store.mennomedia.org/p-264-i-travelled-to-ireland.aspx

DEO in Denver:
http://store.mennomedia.org/p-257-deo-in-denver.aspx

Missional: More than a Buzz Word
http://missionalchurchnetwork.com/missional-more-than-a-buzz-word-2/

What is Missional Church
http://archives.allelon.org/articles/article.cfm?id=511

They Like Jesus, but not the Church
http://www.amazon.com/They-Like-Jesus-but-Church/dp/0310245907

Searching for God knows what
http://www.amazon.com/Searching-Knows-What-Donald- Miller/dp/0785263713

VOCATION (SESSIONS 6 AND 7) EASY READ.

Palmer, Parker J. *Let Your Life Speak: Listening for the Voice of Vocation.* San
    Francisco: Jossey-Bass, 1999.

SHORT-TERM SERVICE OPPORTUNITIES

Mennonite Mission Network (Mennonite Church USA)

A unique approach to short-term mission . . .

We work with local Christian faith communities before our service participants are placed there, so we can be sure our participants are working hand-in-hand with an already-established community. We also encourage the communities to challenge the participants and offer them new perspective, so that both groups are blessed by each other.

Yearlong community-based opportunities:

- **Mennonite Voluntary Service** provides opportunities for people 20 years and older to live out their faith through service in communities across the United States.
- **Service Adventure** promotes service, learning and spiritual growth for post-high school adults in seven U.S. cities.
- **Radical Journey** invites young adults (ages 18-25) to faith formation and leadership development in a variety of cross-cultural settings.
- **DOOR: Dwell** gives individuals 18-30 years old an opportunity to be part of God's transforming work in the city as they test and prepare for a long-term call to urban ministry.

Service and learning opportunities for groups:

- **DOOR (Discovering Opportunities for Outreach and Reflection)** allows youth groups to immerse themselves in city life, encounter the living urban church, serve in community-based ministries, and reflect on the message of the psalmist: "God is in the midst of the city" (Psalm 46:5) by serving for a week in one of six urban locations.

Individual short-term opportunities:

- **SOOP** gives short-term service opportunities to adults and families—a partnership with Mennonite Association of Retired Persons and Mennonite Central Committee Canada.
- **Youth Venture** is a one- to three-week short-term service-learning experience for youth (ages 14-25) in North America or internationally.

For program details, locations, and new opportunities
visit **www.Service.MennoniteMission.net**
or e-mail **Service@MennoniteMission.net**

Mennonite
Church
Canada

SHORT-TERM SERVICE OPPORTUNITIES

MENNONITE CHURCH CANADA WITNESS

Interested in living, learning and serving the church in Canada or in international settings? Why not consider a short-term assignment with Mennonite Church Canada?

INTERNATIONALLY

Interns: MC Canada Witness invites young adults over the age of 18 to serve the church in a variety of settings. Interns usually serve in places where there are also long-term Witness workers. MC Canada interns have served in Hong Kong, Philippines, Thailand, China, Korea, South Africa, Benin, Botswana, Burkina Faso, Bolivia, and Colombia. Assignments may involve teaching, administrative assistance, or helping Witness partners with whatever gifts the intern may have. In addition to service, internship assignments are for learning about oneself and the role of the church in the world. An educational component of reading and reporting will assist the internship participant in reflecting on the impact of their mission involvement and whether they are called to longer-term cross-cultural service through the church.

University/College practicum: If you are a university or college student, why not consider doing your practicum through MC Canada Witness? Talk with your school's practicum director.

Radical Journey: For those interested in a group experience, Radical Journey is offered through MC Canada in cooperation with Mennonite Mission Network (Mennonite Church USA). Radical Journey is a one-year program that involves an orientation month, 10 months of international service, and an integration month in the participants home congregation. Sites have included Paraguay, South Africa, and England.

IN CANADA

Mennonite Voluntary Service Adventure (MVSA) provides an opportunity for young adults to serve and live together in one of four local units across Canada. Participants volunteer in local non-profit agencies in partnership with a sponsoring congregation. Volunteers have served in medical clinics, tutored children, worked with senior citizens, repaired old housing, and helped meet the needs of poor people in various locations; check the following: www.mvsa.net/.

HOW TO GET INVOLVED

For more information or to request an application form, call the Human Resources office at MC Canada toll-free at 1-866-888-6785, extension 110. When you are online, explore the MC Canada website at www.mennonitechurch.ca/serve.

Give us a call. Let's explore the possibility of short-term service!